gudetama™

adulting for the lazy

ONI PRESS

Sanrio®

written, illustrated, and lettered
by
wook-jin clark

Color flats by Jason Fischer

Edited by Sarah Gaydos
Designed by Kate Z. Stone & Sonja Synak

gudetama™

adulting for the lazy

ONI PRESS

Sanrio®

Published by Oni-Lion Forge Publishing Group, LLC

James Lucas Jones, president & publisher • Sarah Gaydos, editor in chief
Charlie Chu, e.v.p. of creative & business development • Brad Rooks, director of operations
Amber O'Neill, special projects manager • Harris Fish, events manager
Margot Wood, director of marketing & sales • Devin Funches, sales & marketing manager
Katie Sainz, marketing manager • Tara Lehmann, marketing & publicity associate
Troy Look, director of design & production • Kate Z. Stone, senior graphic designer
Sonja Synak, graphic designer • Hilary Thompson, graphic designer
Sarah Rockwell, junior graphic designer • Angie Knowles, digital prepress lead
Vincent Kukua, digital prepress technician • Jasmine Amiri, senior editor • Shawna Gore, senior editor
Amanda Meadows, senior editor • Robert Meyers, senior editor, licensing • Grace Bornhoft, editor
Zack Soto, editor • Chris Cerasi, editorial coordinator • Steve Ellis, vice president of games
Ben Eisner, game developer • Michelle Nguyen, executive assistant • Jung Lee, logistics coordinator

Joe Nozemack, publisher emeritus

ONI PRESS

1319 SE Martin Luther King, Jr. Blvd. Suite 240
Portland, OR 97214

onipress.com **lionforge.com**
onipress lionforge

sanrio.com
gudetama
gudetamatweets
gudetama

wookjinclark.com
wookjinclark

gudetama™ by Sanrio®

First Edition: August 2020

Retail ISBN 978-1-62010-739-3
Oni Exclusive Variant ISBN 978-1-62010-837-6
eISBN 978-1-62010-740-9

1 2 3 4 5 6 7 8 9 10

Library of Congress Control Number
2020931956

Printed in South Korea through
Four Colour Print Group, Louisville, KY.

Retail Cover by Wook-Jin Clark
Oni Exclusive Variant Cover by Derek Charm

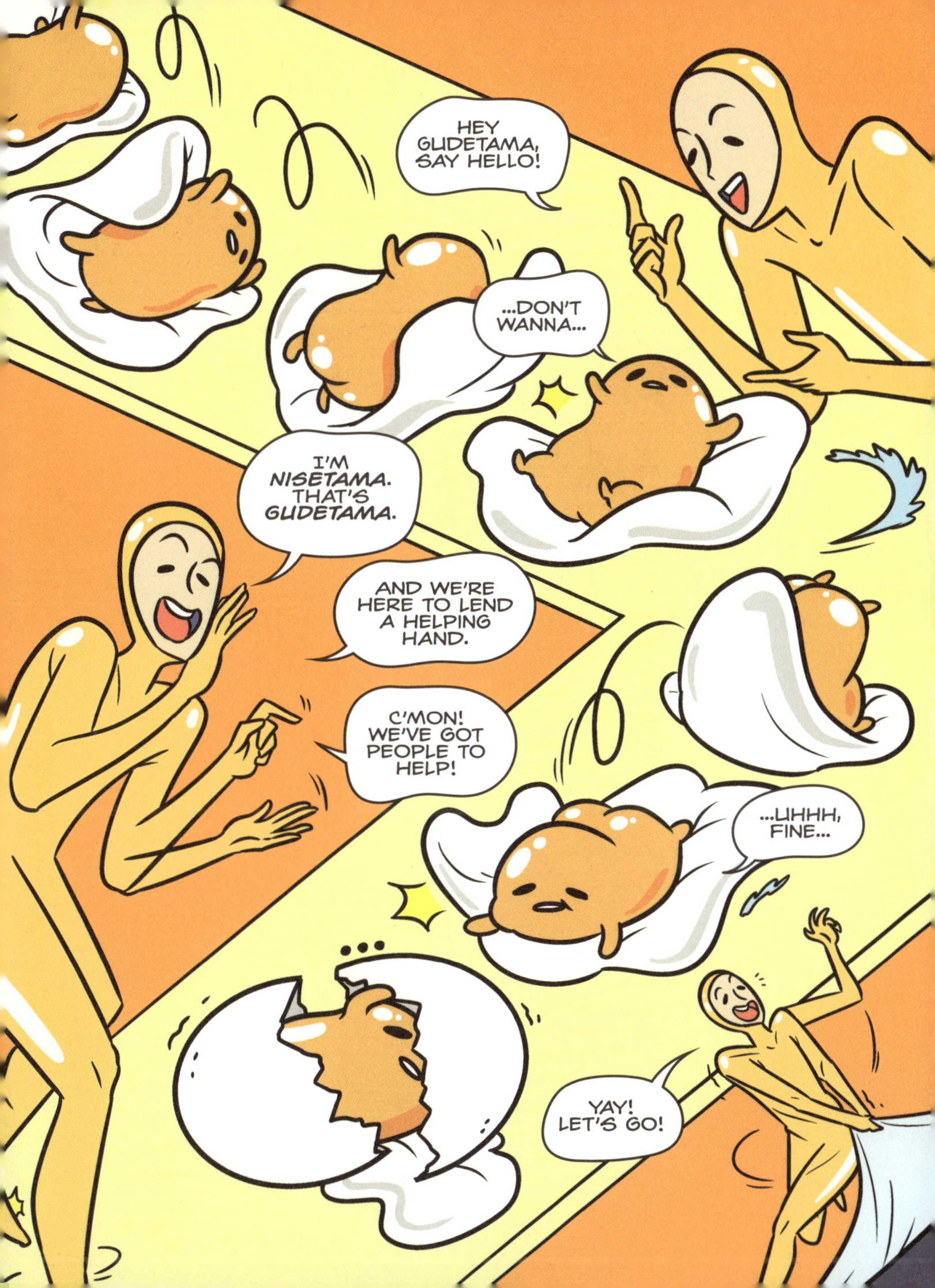
HEY GUDETAMA, SAY HELLO!
...DON'T WANNA...
I'M *NISETAMA*. THAT'S *GUDETAMA*.
AND WE'RE HERE TO LEND A HELPING HAND.
C'MON! WE'VE GOT PEOPLE TO HELP!
...UHHH, FINE...
YAY! LET'S GO!

WOOO!
FREEDOM!
WHAT'S WRONG?
THIS IS THE FIRST DAY OF THE REST OF YOUR LIFE.
I SHOULD BE HAPPY RIGHT NOW, BUT ALL I CAN THINK ABOUT IS THE MASSIVE STUDENT LOAN DEBT I HAVE NOW!
...SURE...
...BUT YOU DON'T HAVE TO START PAYING THEM BACK FOR SIX MONTHS.
WAIT... WHAT?
WELL, THAT IS TRUE, BUT IT'S STILL GOOD TO START THINKING ABOUT THEM NOW BEFO--
STOP TALKING!
THAT'S A PROBLEM FOR FUTURE RHONDA!
AHAHAHA
MUAHAHAHA
FOR NOW, I'M UNSTOPPABLE!
end.

EWWW!! NOOOOO!!
NOO!
AAARRGHH!!
?
I SAID NOOOO!!
MY TUMMY!
IT HURTS!
C'MON, BABE, YOU JUST GOTTA EAT A LITTLE BIT AND IT'LL GO AWAY.
I SAID NO! I HATE SALADS!
YOU CAN'T MAKE ME EAT IT!
WHAT'S THE PROBLEM?
UGHH, I KNOW I NEED VEGGIES TO SURVIVE, BUT IT IS SO *BORING* AND *GREEN* AND NOT CHICKEN NUGGETS.

I JUST REALLY HATE THE TEXTURE... HOW IT FEELS IN MY MOUTH!
...
WELL...
I THINK I'VE GOT A SOLUTION.
OKAY...
WE'LL TAKE THE SALAD, ADD SOME TASTY FRUITS...
NOW YOU CAN GET SOME HEALTHY STUFF AS JUICE...
IT SHOULD BE EASIER GOING DOWN.
I DUNNO ABOUT THIS.
IT'S A MILKSHAKE, BUT NOT.
AND YOU'LL HAVE LESS TUMMY ISSUES...
JUST GIVE IT A TRY.
FINE.

BLEEGH...
I HATE THIS!
THIS ISN'T FAIR! I SHOULD BE ABLE TO EAT LIKE I DID IN HIGH SCHOOL.
MA! ONLY PIZZA!
AND MEATY ONES, TOO! VEGGIES ON PIZZA SUCK!
VEGGIES?!
NO ONE EATS VEGGIES IN THE MORNING! PREPOSTEROUS!
WELL, HOW LONG HAS IT BEEN SINCE HIGH SCHOOL?

WELCOME BACK!
20 YEAR REUNION
?
...OH.
WELL, BETTER LATE THAN NEVER.
end.

GUDETAMA, I DON'T KNOW WHAT TO DO!
I'VE BEEN TOLD A RUMOR ABOUT MY FRIEND MILES, AND IF IT'S TRUE, I DUNNO IF I CAN STILL BE FRIENDS WITH HIM.
SHOULD I ASK HIM?
WHAT IF IT'S NOT TRUE?
I WANNA BE A GOOD FRIEND BU--
STOP.
FIRST, RATE THE "RUMOR."
ON A SCALE OF ONE TO TEN, WHERE DOES IT LAND?
9
8
7
6
5
4
3
2
1
RUMOR HAS IT
ONE BEING "OH, THAT? PFFT, WHATEVER."
TEN BEING "WE AREN'T FRIENDS ANYMORE."
IF IT'S A THREE OR BELOW, JUST KEEP IT TO YOURSELF.
IF IT'S A SEVEN OR ABOVE, TALKING TO THEM IS A SAFER BET. GET IT OUT THERE.
HMM... I'D SAY MAYBE A SIX?
6
5
FOR THOSE MID-LEVEL RUMORS, WE NEED TO CONSULT "*THE WHEEL*"!

THE WAY YOU ANSWER THESE "YES" OR "NO" QUESTIONS WILL DETERMINE WHETHER YOU SHOULD TALK TO YOUR FRIEND MILES.
DOES THIS SOUND LIKE SOMETHING YOUR FRIEND MILES WOULD DO?
NO.
WOULD YOU WANT TO KNOW IF SOMEONE SAID THIS ABOUT YOU?
YES.
DO YOU TRUST WHERE THE INFORMATION IS COMING FROM?
...WELLLL?
UGH. I'M TIRED, THIS QUESTION IS TOO LONG.
YOU'VE GOT TWO CHOICES.
ONE, TALK TO MILES LIKE A GOOD FRIEND.
TWO, DON'T TELL HIM AND LIVE IN A FRIENDSHIP WITHOUT TRUST.

I THINK I KNOW WHAT I NEED TO DO.
IF THE RUMOR'S TRUE, I KNOW WE CAN TALK IT OUT.
THANKS, I FEEL A LOT BETTER NOW.
TAP TAP
MILES
YOU FREE IN A BIT? I GOTTA ASK YOU SOMETHING.
ONE HOUR LATER.
HEY MAN, IS EVERYTHING COOL? YOUR TEXT SOUNDED URGENT.
THINGS ARE GOOD, I JUST WANTED TO ASK YOU SOMETHING...
SURE, WHAT'S UP?
IS IT TRUE YOU FARTED AT MY POETRY READING LAST WEEK...
...AND THEN BLAMED IT ON THE BARISTA?
AW MAN, MY BAD! I'M SORRY I DIDN'T TELL YOU. I HAD A HUGE MEAL RIGHT BEFORE YOUR READING AND RAN TO MAKE IT ON TIME. I DIDN'T WANNA MISS IT!
I DUNNO IF THAT WAS A SIX... MORE LIKE A TWO.
REALLY? I DEFINITELY HAD THAT AS A NINE IN MY BOOK.
end.

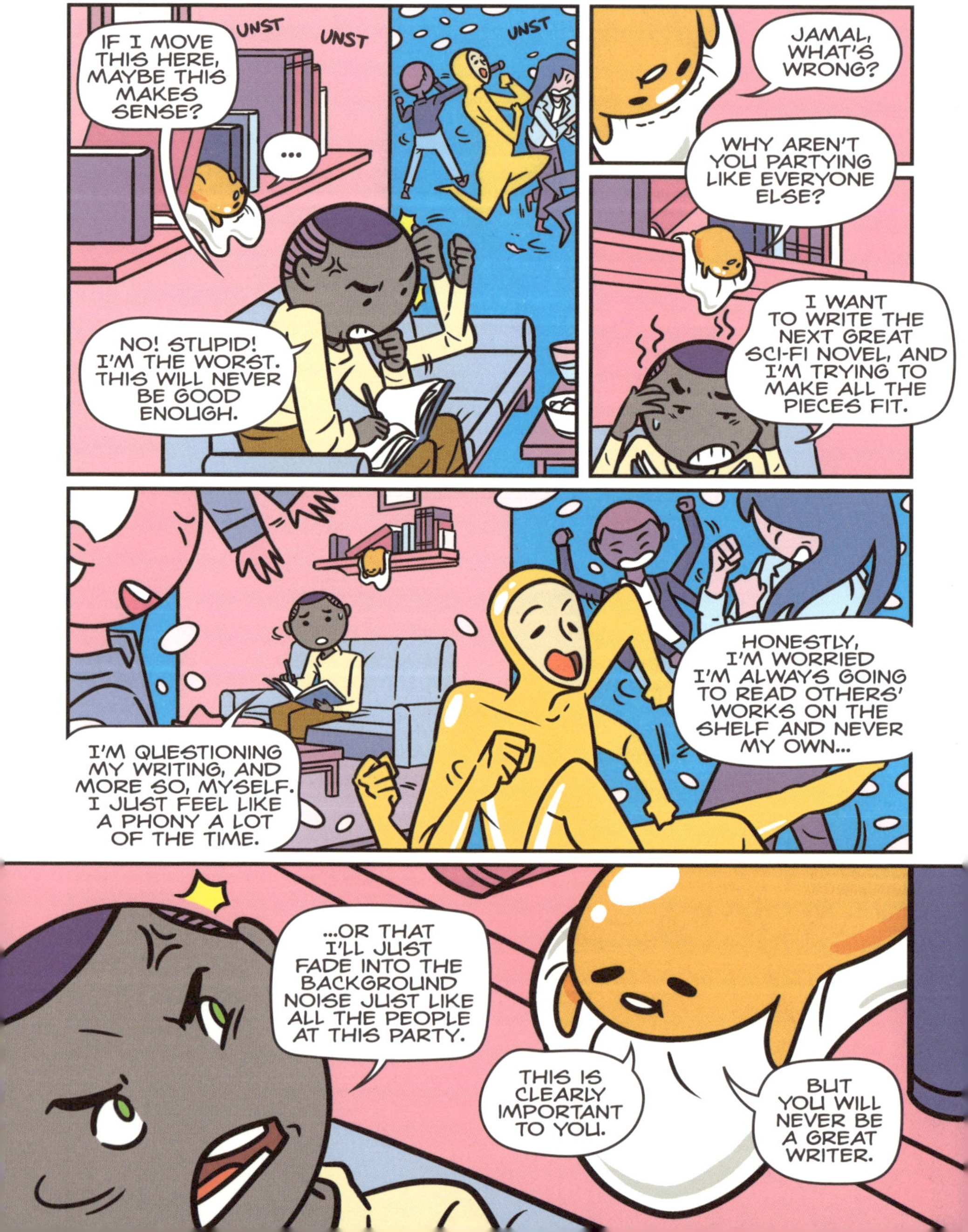
IF I MOVE THIS HERE, MAYBE THIS MAKES SENSE?
UNST
UNST
UNST
...
NO! STUPID! I'M THE WORST. THIS WILL NEVER BE GOOD ENOUGH.
JAMAL, WHAT'S WRONG?
WHY AREN'T YOU PARTYING LIKE EVERYONE ELSE?
I WANT TO WRITE THE NEXT GREAT SCI-FI NOVEL, AND I'M TRYING TO MAKE ALL THE PIECES FIT.
I'M QUESTIONING MY WRITING, AND MORE SO, MYSELF. I JUST FEEL LIKE A PHONY A LOT OF THE TIME.
HONESTLY, I'M WORRIED I'M ALWAYS GOING TO READ OTHERS' WORKS ON THE SHELF AND NEVER MY OWN...
...OR THAT I'LL JUST FADE INTO THE BACKGROUND NOISE JUST LIKE ALL THE PEOPLE AT THIS PARTY.
THIS IS CLEARLY IMPORTANT TO YOU.
BUT YOU WILL NEVER BE A GREAT WRITER.

WHAT THE HECK, MAN?! I JUST OPENED UP TO YOU AND YOU JUS--
...STOP.
I WASN'T FINISHED.
YOU WILL NEVER BE A GREAT WRITER...
...UNTIL YOU FIRST BECOME A GREAT JAMAL.
...
TH-THANK YOU... THAT WAS BEAUTIFU--
WAIT, THAT'S IT!
?
THAT'S IT!
AND THEN SHE CAN--
WHICH WILL HELP LEAD TO THE--
AND DROPS LOADS OF--
EVERYTHING GOOD OVER HERE?
MEH... I GUESS. WHO KNOWS, REALLY.

IN THE NOT-SO-DISTANT FUTURE...
OPEN
Lehu BOOKS
A SIGNING W/ JAMAL
...I THINK I KNOW THAT GUY...
WELL LET'S GO IN, THEN!
NAH. IT LOOKS PACKED. LET'S SEE WHAT WE CAN HEAR FROM OUT HERE.
ONE JAMAL TO RULE THEM ALL!
"ONE MAN WILL STOP AT NOTHING TO DEFEAT ALL HIS CLONES AND ALTERNATE-REALITY SELVES IN THE EPIC FINALE TO THE JAMAL WARS TRILOGY!"
THAT'S NOT REALLY WHAT I MEANT BY BEING THE BEST YOU YOU CAN BE...
BUT... WHATEVER WORKS, I GUESS...

end.

I'VE HIT ROCK BOTTOM, GUDETAMA.
SO MUCH HAS GONE WRONG IN THE LAST YEAR.
IT JUST FEELS LIKE I RUIN EVERYTHING I TOUCH.
...WELL, THAT ISN'T TRUE.
THE NICE PART IS, THERE'S ONLY ONE PLACE TO GO. AND THAT'S UP.
STEP ONE: GET BACK IN THE FLOW.
UPSIE-DAISY!
LET'S START WITH THINGS YOU KNOW YOU CAN DO AND YOU'VE DONE BEFORE.
JUST TAKE SMALL STEPS.
START SMALL, WITH EASY THINGS TO REMEMBER.
LIKE BRUSHING YOUR TEETH, DRINKING WATER, NOT POOPING ON YOUR LAWN, ETC.
WE ALL NEED TO FEEL LITTLE WINS!
STEP TWO: LITTLE VICTORIES.
LOVE YOUR HAIR TODAY!
I-I DUNNO IF I CAN GO OUT YET!
I'M NOT READY!
SNIP
HONK HONK
HISS
THIS IS A GOOD LEAD-IN TO...

IT'S TOUGH TO GET BACK OUT THERE, BUT KNOW YOU'LL HAVE A SPACE JUST WAITING FOR YOU AT HOME.
LET'S MAKE THIS PLACE A SAFE HAVEN FOR YOU!
STEP THREE: CREATING A SAFE ZONE.
AAH! NOW I NEVER HAVE TO LEAVE!
...WEEELLL...

SOONER OR LATER, YOU'LL HAVE TO LEAVE YOUR SHELL.
DO I HAVE TO?
...PFFT, WHAT?
WHEN YOU'RE READY, YOU'LL KNOW.
I KNOW. YOU'RE RIGHT.
IT'S TIME.
...YES, YOU GO.
I'M GONNA STAY HERE.
BEFORE YOU GO, THERE'S ONE FINAL STEP.
STEP FOUR: DON'T FORGET.
WRITE A LETTER TO YOURSELF.
YOU DON'T WANT TO FORGET THIS FEELING.
IF THERE'S A DAY YOU'RE FEELING BACKED INTO A CORNER AGAIN, PULL OUT THIS LETTER AND READ IT TO YOURSELF.
I CAN DO THIS! I'M BACK!
...I'M STAYING HERE...
...BRING BACK SNACKS.
YES!
end.

EVERYONE LOVES MY TWIN SISTER NOREEN!
WILL I EVER ESCAPE FROM HER SHADOW?
TELL ME MORE...
WE LIKED A LOT OF THE SAME STUFF. WE COMPLIMENTED EACH OTHER WELL.
IT STARTED TO CHANGE IN HIGH SCHOOL...
?
AND NOW IN ADULTHOOD, IT STILL FEELS LIKE A RIFT EXISTS.
NOREEN IS SUPER SUCCESSFUL, AND I'M STILL JUST TRYING TO BREAK INTO MY FIELD.
WE ALL REACH OUR OWN APEX AT DIFFERENT TIMES.
...YEAH, YOU JUST GOTTA BE PATIENT.
I PREFER BEING PATIENT BY TAKING A NAP, THEN STARTING AGAIN.

...I KNOW, YOU'RE RIGHT...
I KNOW I'M NOT MY SISTER.
BUT I'LL FIND WHO I AM, JUST LIKE SHE DID.
WITH TIME AND PATIENCE.
I DON'T WANNA BE A UNICORN LIKE NOREEN.
...WHA?!
I'M A TIGER!
A POWERFUL LOOK!
Y-YOU LOOK AMAZING!!
ALSO, WHAT?!
I COULD HAVE BEEN A TIGER?!
WAIT, YOU THINK I LOOK COOL?
I THOUGHT YOU HATED ME?
WHAT? YOU'RE MY SISTER, I'LL ALWAYS LOVE YOU. WE DON'T HAVE TO SEE EYE-TO-EYE ON EVERYTHING.
I LOVE THAT WE EACH HAVE OUR OWN THING. THAT'S WHY WE'VE ALWAYS COMPLIMENTED EACH OTHER SO WELL.
WELL, GUDETAMA, WE DID IT AGAIN...
HIBERNATING GO AWAY
end.

I DUNNO WHAT'S WRONG WITH ME, GUDETAMA.
I'M UP FOR A PROMOTION NEXT MONTH, BUT I COULDN'T CARE LESS.
I'M ALWAYS TIRED AND RUNNING ON FUMES.
I DON'T WANNA THROW AWAY AN OPPORTUNITY, BUT I...
DO YOU NEED THIS JOB?
WELL, IT'S GOOD, BUT I DON'T HAVE ANY FREE TIME.
NO, I SAID, DO YOU NEED THIS JOB? LIKE, *REALLY NEED* THIS JOB?
...WELL, I MEAN YES, I HAVE TO PAY MY BILLS AND--
DO YOU SEE YOURSELF HERE IN TEN YEARS FROM NOW?
...UMM...
IMAGINE YOUR BOSS.
NOW IMAGINE YOU AS YOUR BOSS, OR YOUR BOSS' BOSS. CAN YOU PICTURE THAT?
...WELL, NO, NOT REALLY.
THEN I THINK YOU HAVE YOUR ANSWER.
CASE CLOSED. ON TO THE NEXT ONE...
WAIT! I STILL NEED HELP, HERE!
FROM WHAT IT SOUNDS LIKE, THIS IS JUST A JOB AND NOT YOUR CAREER, OR CALLING.

A JOB
A MEANS TO AN END. YOU WORK BECAUSE IT PROVIDES THE MONEY YOU NEED TO SURVIVE. THERE'S LESS INVESTMENT ON YOUR PART.
A CALLING
WORK YOU LOVE THAT IS LESS CLOUDED WITH THE THOUGHT OF MAKING MONEY FROM IT. IT IS PURELY PLEASURE FOR ITS OWN SAKE. IT'S SOMETHING YOU LIVE, BREATHE, AND SLEEP.
A CAREER
WORK YOU SEE YOURSELF DOING FOR THE LONG HAUL. IT'S A JOB THAT YOU CAN SEE A FUTURE FOR YOURSELF IN. YOU'RE INVESTED.
EACH OF THESE CAN MORPH INTO ANOTHER.
A JOB CAN BECOME A CAREER, WHICH CAN BECOME A CALLING. BUT THEY WON'T ALWAYS TURN INTO THE OTHER.
WHAT'S SOMETHING YOU LOVE?
I LIKE TO DESIGN CLOTHES...
...FOR MY DOGS.
• • •
...OKAY, I THINK I CAN WORK WITH THAT.
AHH! SO CUTE!
I LOVE THEM!
THANKS!
ARE YOU SELLING THESE?
HERE AND THERE, BUT NOT ENOUGH TO MAKE A LIVING.

I LOVE MAKING THESE. I WOULD DO IT ALL THE TIME, BUT THEY JUST TAKE TOO LONG TO MAKE.
I COULD MAKE THEM FASTER, BUT THEY WOULDN'T BE AS GOOD.
IS THERE A WAY TO DO BOTH JOBS AND NOT OVERWHELM YOURSELF?
hmm...
I'VE GOT IT!
MIA DESERVES THIS PROMOTION. SHE PUT IN THE HARD WORK AND TIME!
ALSO, I'M DROPPING DOWN TO PART-TIME.
PHEW! YOU BOTH DESERVE THIS PROMOTION, AND I DIDN'T KNOW WHO I WAS GONNA CHOOSE!
THIS JUST SEEMED LIKE THE RIGHT MOVE.
I KNOW I CAN'T GO FULL-TIME YET AS A CANINE CLOTHING DESIGNER...
BUT NOW I'M DEVOTING MORE TIME AND ENERGY TOWARD MAKING MY DREAM A REALITY.
THAT WAS A REALLY MATURE DECISION.
OR YOU COULD JUST START MAKING YOUR DOGS PAY RENT...
...FREELOADERS.
end.

I GOT LETTERS FROM A BUNCH OF PEOPLE AT THIS OFFICE THAT NEED OUR HELP...
...SO I THOUGHT WE COULD MAKE OUR ROUNDS AND HELP AS WE GO!
...AS LONG AS I DON'T HAVE TO MOVE.
AWAY WE GO!
PSST! HEY.
!
MY BOSS HATES ME, BUT MY BOSS' BOSS LOVES ME.
I CAN FEEL THE HATE IN HIS GLARE.

WHY ARE YOU WORRIED?
YOU'RE GOOD... UNTIL YOUR BOSS' BOSS RETIRES.
THEN RUN.
I HAVE TO HAVE AN UNCOMFORTABLE CONVERSATION WITH A COWORKER.
HOW SHOULD I DO IT?
GO TO HR, THEN YOU DON'T HAVE TO.
OR LEAVE THEM AN OMINOUS NOTE.
I KNOW WHAT YOU DID...
SOMEONE KEEPS STEALING MY FOOD FROM THE FRIDGE.
KAY
TIM
HOW CAN I CATCH THEM?
ROY
FILL A BURRITO WITH TOOTHPASTE AND PUT IT IN THE FRIDGE.
WAIT FOR SOMEONE TO RUN OUT DISGUSTED.
HEH...
ROY
THEN YOU'LL KNOW WHO IT IS.

HELP!
I HAVE TO FART AND I'M STUCK IN A MEETING.
DO YOU LIKE THE PEOPLE YOU WORK WITH?
IF YES, ASK TO LEAVE.
IF NOT, LET 'ER RIIIIIP.
IS THERE A RIGHT WAY TO ASK FOR A PROMOTION?
JUST DO IT.
IF NOTHING HAPPENS, WAIT THREE MONTHS AND THEN REPEAT.
HOW MANY TIMES HAVE YOU ASKED?
THIS WILL BE MY FOURTH TIME...
AND NOW YOU CAN GO FORTH...
...TO A NEW JOB.

I THINK I'M GOING TO GET FIRED!
WHAT MAKES YOU THINK THAT?
WELL, I KEEP STEALING THINGS.
AND EATING OTHER PEOPLE'S FOOD.
I JUST WANNA FEEL ALIVE!
AND I CAN'T STOP!
...OKAY.
MAYBE YOU SHOULD TRY "FEELING ALIVE" NOT DURING WORK HOURS.
I DUNNO IF I CAN!
AND I DON'T THINK I WANNA STOP!
NO ONE CAN STOP ME!
SECURITY
I THINK THEY PROLLY WILL...

I'M AN INTERN, HOW CAN I GET A JOB HERE?
WITH HARD WORK AND PATIENCE!
OR...
YOU CAN JUST WAIT ABOUT AN HOUR.
THERE'S PROLLY GONNA BE A FEW OPEN SLOTS HERE, SOON.
NO! NO! NO! NO!
NO! NO! NO! NO!
RESUME
BOSS
HEYA BOSS, GOT A MINUTE?
AHH! NOTHING LIKE A HARD DAY'S WORK, AM I RIGHT?
YOU GAVE SOME GREAT ADVICE TODAY, GUDETAMA!
PLEASE... STOP TALKING...
...YOU'RE TOO LOUD...
end.

SHUT UP! NO WAY!
TOO LOUD...
WHAT'S THE PROBLEM?
MY FRIEND RAYRAY TEXTED ME AND THAT THERES THIS PARTY THAT WILL BE AT BUT NO REALLY WANTS TO BUT IF I DON'T GO EVERYONE WILL WASN'T THERE CAN'T HAVE THAT BECAUSE THEN I'LL ALL MY CRED WITH
...SLOWER ...AND... ...SHORTER.

HELP! HUGE FOMO RN!
...?
...WHAT DAT?
FEAR OF MISSING OUT!
PFFT. JUST SAY NO.
...HEH. THERE'S NOTHING BETTER THAN SAYING NO.
IT'S ONE OF MY FAVORITE THINGS.
HERE, WATCH.
?
NISETAMA, ASK ME TO DO THAT THING YOU'VE ALWAYS WANTED US TO DO.
!!!
ARE YOU SERIOUS?!
WILL YOU GO WITH ME TO THE AMU--
...NO.

...AHHH.
YOU REALLY CAN'T BEAT THAT FEELING.
NOW YOU GIVE IT A TRY--
WOW, YOU'RE RIGHT!
THAT FELT GREAT!
...I'M SO HAPPY FOR YOU...
end.

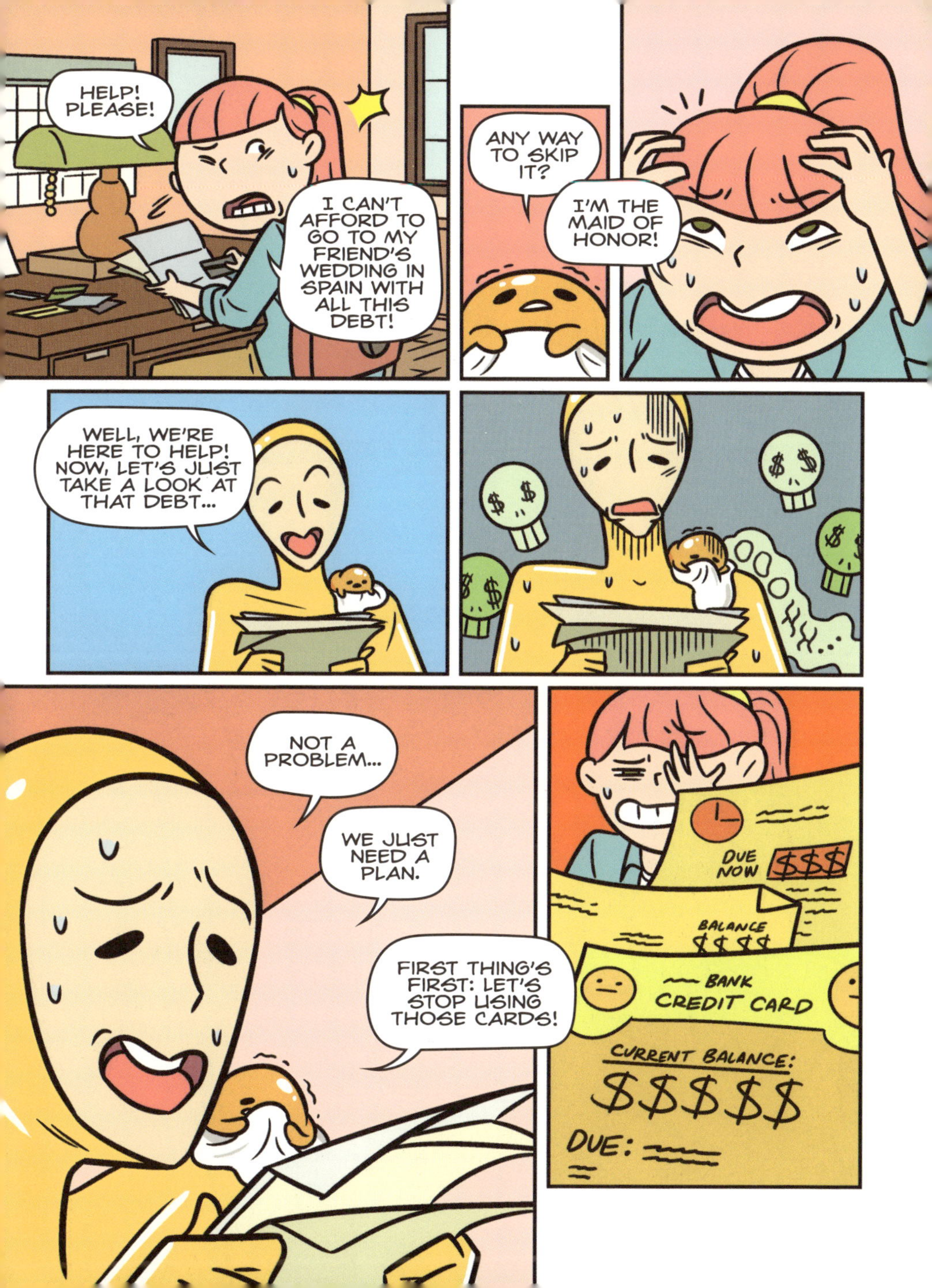
HELP! PLEASE!
I CAN'T AFFORD TO GO TO MY FRIEND'S WEDDING IN SPAIN WITH ALL THIS DEBT!
ANY WAY TO SKIP IT?
I'M THE MAID OF HONOR!
WELL, WE'RE HERE TO HELP! NOW, LET'S JUST TAKE A LOOK AT THAT DEBT...
OOOHH...
NOT A PROBLEM...
WE JUST NEED A PLAN.
FIRST THING'S FIRST: LET'S STOP USING THOSE CARDS!
DUE NOW $$$
BALANCE $$$$
BANK CREDIT CARD
CURRENT BALANCE: $$$$$
DUE:

GOODBYE, OLD FRIENDS...
...OKAY. THAT WAS A BIT OVER-THE-TOP.
YOU COULD'VE JUST THROWN THEM IN THE FREEZER, BUT YOU DO YOU.
SO NOW, LET'S MAKE A BUDGET!
LET'S SEE HOW MUCH YOU MAKE.
AND HOW MUCH TO SAVE FOR YOUR FRIEND'S WEDDING.
HOW MUCH DO YOU NEED EACH MONTH TO LIVE ON?
LIKE THIS MUCH?
PROLLY ABOUT THIS MUCH, FOR SURE.

YOU ACTUALLY MAKE QUITE A BIT, MONTHLY.
WHERE IS ALL THE MONEY GOING?
I THINK I KNOW WHERE IT'S GOING.
YOU'RE NOT BUYING ANYTHING *BIG* EACH MONTH, BUT YOU ARE BUYING A *LOT* OF SMALL THINGS EACH DAY.
WEEELLLL... I DO LIKE TO TREAT MYSELF A BIT...BUT NOTHING OUTLANDISH.
WELL, LET'S JUST SEE HOW MUCH YOU TREAT YOURSELF.
NOTHING WRONG WITH TREATING YOURSELF.
NEW
LET'S SEE WHAT WE CAN CUT DOWN ON AND PUT THAT TOWARD YOUR TRIP.
IT'S PROLLY MORE THAN YOU THINK.

YAY! LET'S GOOO!
ALRIGHT, LET'S DO THIS, I GUESS...
COFFEE
7 A.M.
FIRST THINGS FIRST, MAMA NEEDS HER COFFEE.
WHY?!
WHEN I BROUGHT A THERMOS!
COFFEE IS COFFEE.
THAT FANCY STUFF IS THE SAME AS THIS, BUT THIS IS A LOT CHEAPER.
12 P.M.
AH! THE BEST PART OF MY DAY!
LUNCH TIME!
WHAT TO CHOOSE, WHAT TO CHOOSE!
WE PACKED YOU A LUNCH.
IT'S BOTH CHEAPER AND BETTER FOR YOU!
6 P.M.
BOOK STORE
GASP! THE NEW JAMAL BOOK!
HOLD ON A SEC...
I KNEW YOU LOVED THAT SERIES...
LIBRARY CARD
...SO I BORROWED IT FROM THE LIBRARY FOR YOU, ALREADY!

IF YOU CAN, TRY TAKING PUBLIC TRANSIT OR CARPOOL TO WORK.
AND IF YOU'RE REALLY CLOSE, MAYBE BIKE THERE!
AND TAKE A REUSABLE WATER BOTTLE INSTEAD OF BUYING THEM.
MEAL PREP CAN CUT DOWN ON A LOT OF WEEKLY COSTS.
AND IT'LL SAVE YOU TIME AND ENERGY LATER IN YOUR WEEK...
M
T
W
TH
FREE DAY
FRI
WE ALL NEED TO HAVE CHEAT DAYS, TOO.
GUDETAMA'S RULES WHEN SHOPPING:
1. PICK IT UP
2. WALK AROUND WITH IT FOR 10 MINUTES
3. PUT IT BACK
CHANCES ARE, YOU DIDN'T NEED IT.
I HAVE TO HAVE THIS!
I WANT THIS!
DO I NEED THIS?
I COULD BUY THIS, OR I COULD--
MEH, I THINK I'LL WAIT, FOR NOW...
TOLD YA...

YOU CAN ALSO MAKE EXTRA INCOME IF YOU WANNA SAVE, OR SLASH YOUR DEBT FASTER.
REALLY? HOW?!
BABY-SITTING
BUSKING
RIDE SHARE
DOG WALKING
YOU CAN ALSO SELL STUFF ONLINE OR AT A GARAGE SALE!
SOLD
...I DON'T REALLY NEED TWO EPIC BLADES...
WHOA! YOU'RE SELLING THESE?!

CANCEL ALL SUBSCRIPTION-BASED SERVICES YOU DON'T USE.
NO GUILT, JUST BE HONEST!
GYM
I DUNNO ABOUT THIS...
SAVING MONEY WITH FRIENDS CAN BE FUN, TOO.
INVITE FRIENDS OVER FOR POTLUCK DINNERS.
DO A CLOTHING SWAP WITH FRIENDS! IT'S A FREE WAY TO GET A NEW WARDROBE.
1
2
3
HOST GROUP WORKOUTS INSTEAD OF PAYING FOR GYM MEMBERSHIPS.

AND YOU CAN STILL TREAT YOURSELF...
YOU CAN HAVE FUN! JUST SPEND IN MODERATION.
GIVE YOURSELF AN ALLOWANCE.
I DO, AND IT'S ONLY FOR THINGS I WANT.
$$
I HAVE TO USE THIS WISELY.
AAH.
HERE'S YOUR CHANGE.
AND WHATEVER YOU DON'T USE, JUST ROLL IT OVER TO THE NEXT WEEK.
ROLL OVER

JEEZ! I DIDN'T REALIZE JUST HOW MUCH I COULD HAVE BEEN SAVING!
DEBT
SAVING
WE TOOK THE MONEY YOU SAVED AND SPLIT IT BETWEEN YOUR DEBT AND SAVING FOR THE WEDDING.
I NEVER REALIZED HOW LITTLE I REALLY NEEDED.
THIS FEELS ...GOOD...
ONE YEAR LATER.
MADRID.
SO, I STILL HAVE SOME DEBT, BUT I DON'T FEEL LIKE IT'S A BURDEN ANYMORE!
...AND I'M SO HAPPY I WAS ABLE TO MAKE IT HERE FOR YOUR SPECIAL DAY!
JUST GONNA TAKE A FEW OF THESE FOR THE ROAD!
...WE'VE CREATED A MONSTER...
RUN FREE, YOU BEAUTIFUL, MONSTER!
end.

HOW DO I GET MY SON OFF OF HIS PHONE? HE'S ON IT 24/7 AT THE HOUSE!
CHANGE THE PASSWORD EVERY DAY.
AND GIVE IT TO HIM AFTER HE DOES A CHORE.
PASSWORD: JACOB$trashday ♥mom
SHOULD I KEEP A DIARY? I ONLY HEAR GOOD THINGS.
YES. IT'S A SAFE PLACE TO BE BRUTALLY HONEST WITH YOURSELF AND REFLECT.
I HAVE ONE, AND I WRITE ALL MY SECRETS IN IT.
FOR GUDE EYES ONLY!
AND NO ONE WILL EVER SEE IT.
I'VE MOVED TO A NEW CITY, HOW DO I MAKE FRIENDS?
WRITE YOUR NAME AND EMAIL ON A PIECE OF PAPER.
WAD IT UP, AND THROW IT OUT THE WINDOW.
YOU WILL HAVE A FRIEND IN NO TIME.
SEE, TOLD YA.

HOW CAN I LIVE A MINIMALIST LIFESTYLE?
TAKE YOUR PHONE AND ALL YOUR THINGS, PUT THEM IN A BOX WITH "FREE" WRITTEN ON IT, AND PUT IT OUTSIDE.
FREE!
NOW YOU HAVE NOTHING.
YOU DID IT.
YOU'RE WELCOME.
...
SHOULD I GET A CREDIT CARD?
YES, BUT ONLY FOR EMERGENCIES.
LIKE THESE LIMITED, EXCLUSIVE ACTION FIGURES ONLY AVAILABLE ONLINE FOR A SHORT WINDOW OF TIME?
SURE, AS LONG AS YOU'RE COOL...
...WITH THE UNLIMITED WINDOW OF TIME EXCLUSIVELY LIVING WITH YOUR PARENTS.
I WANNA BE LAZY TOO, GUDETAMA!
CAN I BE LAZY WITH YOU?
...SURE, AS LONG AS YOU PAY BILLS AND RENT...
WAIT, WHAT?
NO FREELOADING HERE.

...UHHH, I'M SO TIRED...
...HELPING PEOPLE GROW UP IS A LOT OF WORK.
THAT SOUNDS A LITTLE WEIRD, DON'T YOU THINK?
...SORRY. I'M JUST TIRED.
...FROM THE PITY PARTY...
...OKAY.
GUDETAMA, I THINK "HELPING THEM FIND THEIR WAY" SOUNDS BETTER THAN "GROWING UP" OR "PITY PARTY."
...SURE, LET'S GO WITH THAT.
CAN I SLEEP NOW?
LET'S CLOCK OUT!
'TIL NEXT TIME!
end.

wook jin clark

was born in South Korea and raised in South Carolina. He loves coffee, doodling, walking around, and COFFEE!! Look for his work in Image Comic's *Flavor,* Boom's *Bee and Puppycat, Regular Show, Adventure Time,* and *Bravest Warriors* comics.

making of gudetama™

adulting for the lazy

by Wook-Jin Clark

It all starts out with a script!

PAGE 1: *Introduction Page with Gudetama and Nisetama Introducing themselves again, just like in GUDETAMA: LOVE FOR THE LAZY.*

Panel 1: *Close up shot of Gudetama rolling.*

Panel 2: *Close up shot of Nisetama speaking to Gudetama.*

Nisetama: Hey Gudetama, say hello!

Panel 3: *Gudetama still rolling.*

Gudetama: ...don't wanna...

Panel 4: *Small panel of Nisetama introducing himself.*

Nisetama: I'm Nisetama. That's Gudetama.
Nisetama: And we're here to lend a helping hand.

Panel 5: *Nisetama speaking to Gudetama who is crawling back into its half broken egg shell.*

Nisetama: C'mon! We've got people to help!
Gudetama: ...uhhh...fine...

Panel 6: *Small corner panel of Nisetama turning the page. Nisetama is excited.*

Nisetama: Yay! Let's go!

And then on to pencils!

Next up, I ink the pages.

And finally, they are colored & lettered!

read more from oni press!

GUDETAMA: LOVE FOR THE LAZY

By Wook-Jin Clark

Dating is exhausting, so let's take a lighthearted approach to exploring it with Gudetama, everyone's favorite grumpy egg!

SCOTT PILGRIM COLOR COLLECTION, VOL. 1

By Bryan Lee O'Malley
with colors by Nathan Fairbairn

The *New York Times* bestselling series and basis for the movie *Scott Pilgrim vs. The World* is now available in a new softcover format!

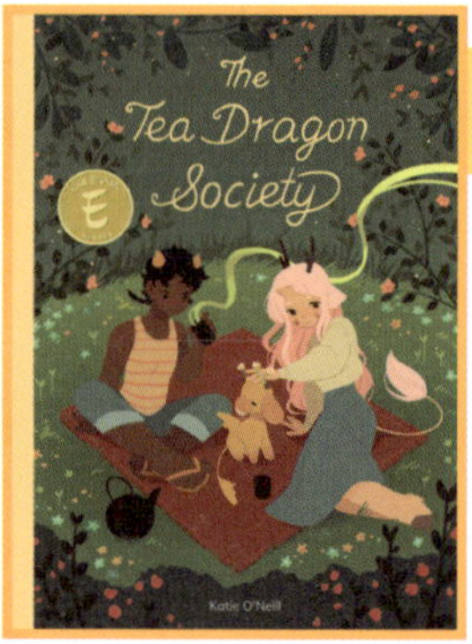

THE TEA DRAGON SOCIETY

By Katie O'Neill

A multiple award-winning, gentle fantasy that follows the story of a blacksmith apprentice and the people she meets as she becomes entwined in the enchanting world of tea dragons.

RICK AND MORTY™, VOL. 1

By Zac Gorman, CJ Cannon
with Ryan Hill and Marc Ellerby

The hit comic book series based on Dan Harmon and Justin Roiland's hilarious [adult swim]™ animated show!

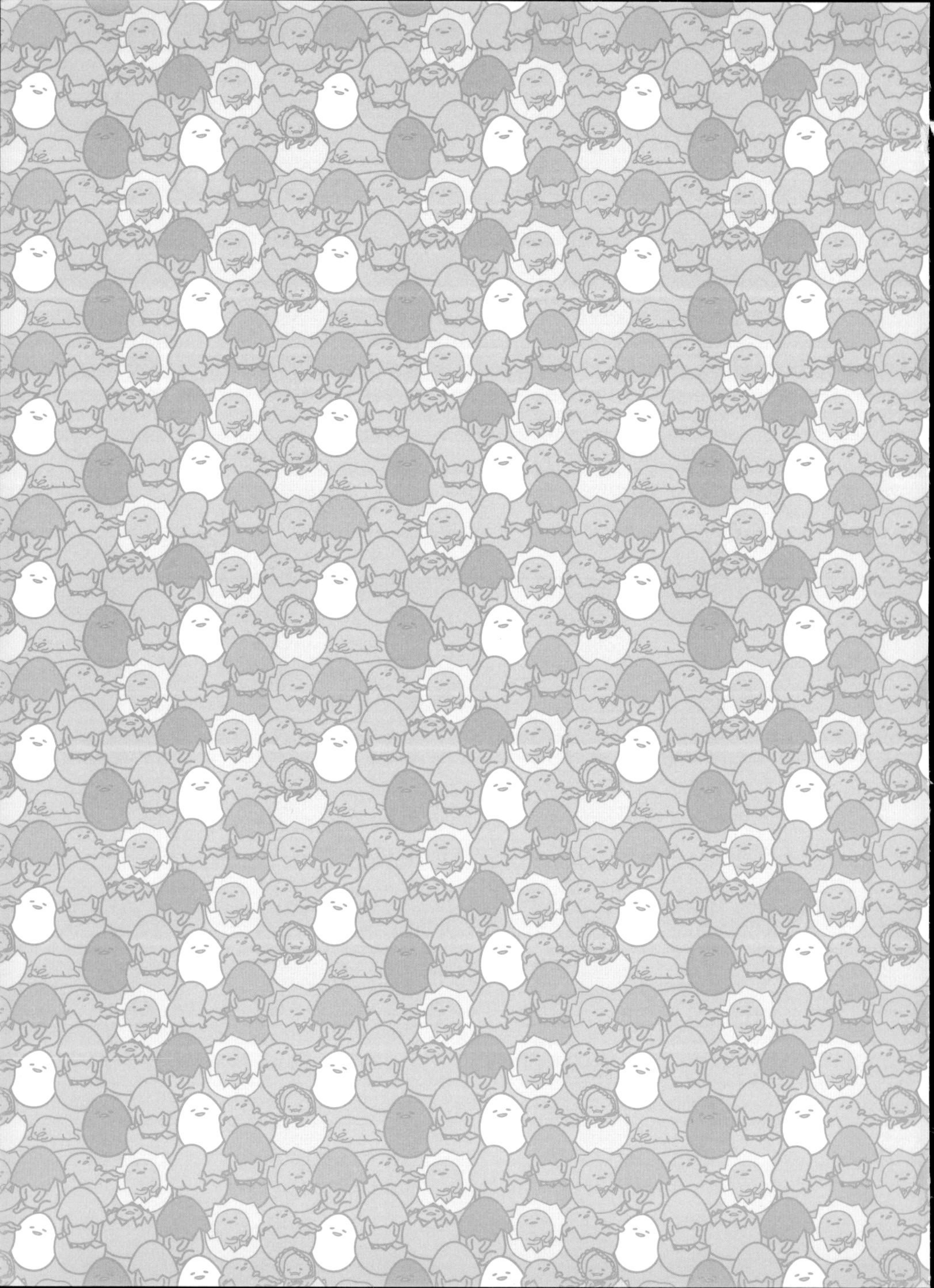